MIRABAI

Selected Titles by Robert Bly

Eating the Honey of Words: New and Selected Poems
The Night Abraham Called to the Stars
The Soul is Here for Its Own Joy:
Sacred Poems from Many Cultures
Kabir: Ecstatic Poems

Selected Titles by Jane Hirshfield

Given Sugar, Given Salt
The Lives of the Heart
Nine Gates: Entering the Mind of Poetry
Women in Praise of the Sacred:
43 Centuries of Spiritual Poetry by Women

MIRABAI

Ecstatic Poems

VERSIONS BY

ROBERT BLY

AND

JANE HIRSHFIELD

BEACON PRESS

Boston

Beacon Press
25 Beacon Street
Boston, Massachusetts 02108-2892
www.beacon.org

Beacon Press books
are published under the auspices of
the Unitarian Universalist Association of Congregations.

07 06 05 04 08 7 6 5 4 3 2 1

This book is printed on acid-free paper that meets the
uncoated paper ANSI/NISO specifications for
permanence as revised in 1992.

Book design by Dean Bornstein

Library of Congress Cataloging-in-Publication Data

Bly, Robert.
  Mirabai : ecstatic poems / versions by Robert Bly and Jane
Hirshfield.— 1st ed.
      p. cm.
  ISBN 0-8070-6386-X (cloth : alk. paper)
  1. Mirabai, fl. 1516-1546—Adaptations. I. Mirabai, fl. 1516-1546.
II. Hirshfield, Jane, 1953- III. Title.

PS3552.L9M57 2005
811'.54—dc22

                            2004019238

CONTENTS

A Few Words about Mirabai · *ix*
Robert Bly

Mirabai's Teachings · *xiii*
Jane Hirshfield

I

The Dancing Energy Came by My House

All I Was Doing Was Breathing · 3
The Dagger · 4
Mira Has Finished with Waiting · 5
It's True I Went to the Market · 6
Mira the Milkmaid · 7
The Fish and the Crocodile · 8
Polish into Gold · 9
A Dream of Marriage · 10
Ankle Bells · 12
The Flute · 13
The Rope of Jasmine Blossoms · 14
His Hair · 15
The Gooseberry Patch · 16
To My Brother-in-Law Rana · 17

Fate Is Strange · *18*
Not Hiding Not Seeking · *19*
Don't Go, Don't Go · *20*
Why Mira Can't Come Back to Her Old House · *21*

II

The Ocean of Separation

The Necklace · *24*
How This Will Go · *25*
The Arrow · *26*
Heading for the Ocean · *27*
Don't Tell Me No, Mother · *28*
Where Did You Go? · *29*
Mira Asks Only to Join with the
Elephants & Parrots · *30*
Mira Is Jasmine · *33*
The Cuckoo Calls a Beloved Who Comes · *34*
Only the Beloved Can Open the Blossoming Spring · *36*
Mira Is Mad with Love · *38*
In All My Lives · *39*
The Door · *40*
The Storm Clouds · *41*

III
Love Has Come Home with the Rains

Mira the Bee · *44*

No Longer Thirsty · *45*

The Coffer with the Poisonous Snake · *46*

Mira the Slave · *47*

Awake to the Name · *48*

The Long Drought Is Over · *50*

Near the Throne · *51*

Drunk for Life · *52*

Water through the Fingers · *53*

Wild Plums Are Sweetest · *56*

Mira Swims Free · *57*

Mira the Barterer · *58*

The Clouds · *59*

To Dance for the Dark One

Is All the Clothing Mira Needs · *60*

Faithfulness · *62*

Mira the Lotus · *63*

The Heat of Midnight Tears · *64*

No More Drought · *66*

Afterword by John Stratton Hawley · *67*

Notes · *97*

Translator Credits · *101*

vii

A FEW WORDS ABOUT MIRABAI

It's hard to know where to start with Mirabai. She is out-
rageous in ten or fifteen ways. With enormous elegance
and an exquisite grace, she moves to abandon her upper
class family, all the social roles for a married woman of
her time, the conservative Hindu religious establishment,
and anyone left over who believes in the middle road.
Without permission from anyone, she takes on Krishna
who, in view of his dark bluish face, could be called the
Dark One:

> My friend, I went to the market and bought the Dark
> One.

She assumes that her family would imagine that she
slipped into the market area by night.

> You claim by night, I claim by day.
> Actually I was beating a drum all the time I was buy-
> ing him.

Some say it wasn't worth it to give up all this power and advantage.

> You say I gave too much; I say too little.
> Actually, I put him on a scale before I bought him.

She gave away her social position, the warmth of a family, the link with a hereditary ruler of her area, and her right to riches.

> What I paid was my social body, my town body, my
> family body, and all my inherited jewels.
> Mirabai says: The Dark One is my husband now.

At this point, she no longer speaks to her family. She turns to Him and says:

> Be with me when I lie down; you promised me this
> is an earlier life.

As soon as we read the first poem by Mirabai, we know we are in the presence of someone who is unworldly. No, someone who is deeply worldly. She knows what this world is like. She married into an aristocratic warrior family. With enormous elegance, she describes how she abandoned her caste, the social roles for a married woman of her time, the conservative religious establishment, and anyone left over who believes in the middle road. Shortly before her own wedding, she insisted on being married to a small statue of Krishna; one might have seen a little trouble ahead in that act. As it turned out, her marriage was brief. Her husband died after three years. She apparently remained living in the castle, threatened by relatives who sent her poisonous snakes. Her teacher, an Untouchable, occasionally came to the small village nearby; she was not to visit him. Apparently she would tie her saris together and climb down the castle wall at night. When she found him, she would wash his old feet and drink the water.

There is no one else exactly like her in the whole history of poetry. Mirabai was born in Rajasthan, India, in 1498, and had a profound influence on the religious life of her time. The intensity of the sort she had appears in every century in India, as it did with Ramakrishna in the nineteenth century. Mirabai's genius encouraged thousands of people in her time to compose ecstatic poems and to sing and to dance them. Many villages treasure

poems that she is said to have left behind in that town.
Her poems are still being sung everywhere in India.

ROBERT BLY

MIRABAI'S TEACHINGS

Mirabai's love affair with the Dark One has spoken for itself for close to five hundred years. What can be added here? First, reading her words, must be your own eyes, ears, and heart. Millions have memorized and sung the poems of Mirabai's passion, each finding in her words some intimate and individual truth, and also some companionship along the path of awakening. To read Mirabai is to awaken more deeply into your own life. In her poems, she calls the Beloved by many names. She names also the listeners and witnesses to her path—"Friend," "Sisters," "Companions," she begins many poems. We are still traveling with her along a northern Indian road lined with dusty palaces and fields awaiting the rains which may or may not come.

Mira's poems sing of ecstatic union, and of the despair that ecstatic union, having once been tasted, can then disappear. Her poems sing of what it is like to see through the colors of the world to their single source, and of what it is like to find that this seemingly infinite vision can vanish. "Return," she asks the Dark One, again and again, in poems that come in all the colors of the human heart. In this, Mirabai's experience is as recognizably grounded in a fully human passion as it is in the realm of spiritual realization. Anyone who has loved beyond reason knows what Mira lived, as anyone who has loved beyond self-interest knows also what Love is.

Mirabai offers in her poems the sheer strength of their beauty, founded in the sharp-edged perception of a person who has opened to her own experience in every dimension. She also offers two central teachings of liberation, each grounded in her fierce and unwavering passion. One is the consummate freedom passion calls up in us, and the other is the surrender of self that passion's fulfillment requires. In these two ways, Mira demonstrates over and over, the lover meets fully and intimately the energies of awakening. And through reading her poems, we begin to discover that these two teachings are not separate.

Mirabai's freedom comes from taking her seat at the feet of Oneness (for the Oneness found amid multiplicity is what Krishna, in all his many names and embodiments, means) and refusing to budge from that place. Neither the conventions of societal expectation nor the words—or the desperate actions—of family, friends, or enemies can touch the untouchable self Mira has made through that single act. She has gone beyond caste, beyond personal ego, beyond caring how she is seen. There is something she knows, and it is all she needs to know; or to breathe, to eat, to drink, or lie down with at night. And so she has become a free person, one who can say, "I have felt the swaying of the elephant's shoulders and now you want me to ride on a jackass? Try to be serious."

Mirabai's surrender to the Dark One is similarly complete, and that completeness is the source of her freedom's strength. When you study the lives of mystics, you see that it is not as we might first have imagined—not, that is, a story of seeking and then finding forever. It is harder than that. The experience of oneness comes and goes. And the departure—Mira's contemporary, St. John of the Cross, famously named it "the Dark Night of the Soul"—is a life-shaking shock. That shock reverberates through many of Mira's poems. Look more closely though, and it becomes clear: longing and grief are simply the other face of a love that depends on nothing outside itself, not even its own reciprocation. When the Beloved is present, Mira loves. When the Beloved is absent, she loves. Desire for the Dark One is the sign of his existence. And so, even in what appears to be abject surrender, Mira is free: the one who chooses. The fruit of what comes from this kind of passion, clarity, and fierceness is held in the poems in this book.

JANE HIRSHFIELD

The Dancing Energy
Came by My House

All I Was Doing Was Breathing

Something has reached out and taken in the beams of
    my eyes.
There is a longing, it is for his body, for every hair of
    that dark body.
All I was doing was being, and the Dancing Energy
    came by my house.
His face looks curiously like the moon, I saw it from
    the side, smiling.
My family says: "Don't ever see him again!" And they
    imply things in a low voice.
But my eyes have their own life; they laugh at rules,
    and know whose they are.
I believe I can bear on my shoulders whatever you
    want to say of me.
Mira says: Without the energy that lifts mountains,
    how am I to live?

The Dagger

The Dark One threw me a glance like a dagger today.

Since that moment, I am insane; I can't find my body.

The pain has gone through my arms and legs, and I
can't find my mind.

At least three of my friends are completely mad.

I know the thrower of daggers well; he enjoys roving
the woods.

The partridge loves the moon; and the lamplight
pulls in the moth.

You know, for the fish, water is precious; without it,
the fish dies.

If he is gone, how shall I live? I can't live without
him.

Go and speak to the dagger-thrower: Say, Mira
belongs to you.

Mira Has Finished with Waiting

O friends on this path,
My eyes are no longer my eyes.
A sweetness has entered through them,
Has pierced through to my heart.
How long did I stand in the house of this body
And stare at the road?
My Beloved is a steeped herb, he has cured me
    for life.
Mira belongs to Giridhara, the One Who Lifts All,
And everyone says she is mad.

It's True I Went to the Market

My friend, I went to the market and bought the
     Dark One.
You claim by night, I claim by day.
Actually, I was beating a drum all the time I was
     buying him.
You say I gave too much; I say too little.
Actually, I put him on a scale before I bought him.
What I paid was my social body, my town body, my
     family body, and all my inherited jewels.
Mirabai says: The Dark One is my husband now.
Be with me when I lie down; you promised me this
     in an earlier life.

Mira the Milkmaid

Friend, look—
She is wandering the pathways and alleys, a pot on
her head.
She is calling, "Who will take the beautiful Dark
One?"
The Gopi has forgotten the name for the curds she
carries
And cries only, "Taste Hari! Taste Hari!"
Mira has given herself to the One Who Takes All,
She is his slave, asking no payment.
The milkmaid has seen his radiant body, and all she
can do now is babble.

The Fish and the Crocodile

When Nand's son with his dark face appeared to me,
I forgot about the world and its duties. I went out of
    my mind.
A crown of peacock feathers opened on his forehead,
And I saw the spot of saffron which made my eyes
    glad.
Light caught on his earring; his hair curls fell over his
    cheek,
Like fish who crawl out of a pond to meet a crocodile.
My Lord has entered the play, and the world is
    amazed.
Mira says: I dedicate myself to every arm and leg of
    this Lord.

Polish into Gold

I give my heart without fear to the Beloved:
As the polish goes into the gold, I have gone into
    him.
Through many lives, I heard only the outer music.
Now the teacher has whispered into my ears,
And familiar ties have gone the way of weak thread.
Mira has met the Energy That Lifts Mountains—
That good luck now is her home.

A Dream of Marriage

In my dreams the Great One married me.

Four thousand people came to the wedding.

My bridegroom was the Lord Brajanath, and in the
dream all the doorways were made royal, and he
held my hand.

In my dream he married me, and fortune came to me.

Mirabai has found the Great Snake Giridhar; she
must have done something good in an earlier life.

Ankle Bells

Mira dances, how can her ankle bells not dance?

"Mira is insane," strangers say that. "The family's
ruined."

Poison came to the door one day; she drank it and
laughed.

I am at Hari's feet; I give him body and soul.

A glimpse of him is water: How thirsty I am for that!

Mira's Lord is the one who lifts mountains, he
removes evil from human life.

Mira's Lord attacks the beings of greed; for safety I
go to him.

The Flute

The song of the flute, O sister, is madness.
I thought that nothing that was not God could
    hold me,
But hearing that sound, I lose mind and body,
My heart wholly caught in the net.
O flute, what were your vows, what is your practice?
What power sits by your side?
Even Mira's Lord is trapped in your seven notes.

The Rope of Jasmine Blossoms

O Nandlal! Come live inside my eyes!

Your crown of peacock feathers, your earrings shaped
like fish,

The red smudge on your forehead—all of them are
lovely!

Your body is beautifully shaped, your face is dark,
your eyes are large.

You have a flute between sweet lips, and a rope of
jasmine blossoms around your neck.

Mirabai says: "This Lord of mine gives joy to the
pure in heart, and watches over the poor."

His Hair

You play the flute well; I love your swing curls and
     your earlocks.
Jasumati, your mother, wasn't she the one
Who washed and combed your beautiful hair?
If you come anywhere near my house,
I will close my sandalwood doors, and lock you in.

Mira's lord is half lion and half man.
She turns her life over to the midnight of his hair.

The Gooseberry Patch

Well, friend, I will praise the dear Lord with my
    singing.
I go out each morning looking for spices, and for a
    glimpse of him.
I'll dance as well in Hari's temple, you'll hear my
    ankle bells.
I'll make the castanets give out his name, and I'll cross
    the ocean of this world.
What is this world? A patch of gooseberry bushes. It
    catches us on the way to the one we love.
The Great Snake Giridhar is Mira's lord; I'll sing
    about him; then I will be home.

To My Brother-in-Law Rana

I don't like your strange, strange world, Rana.

There are no holy men in it, and the people are trash.

I don't wear jewelry anymore; I don't bind my hair.

I've given up darkening my eyelids and doing my hair
the married way.

Mira's Lord is the One Who Lifts Mountains; I don't
need a bridegroom.

Fate Is Strange

Fate is strange.
Look: the deer's eyes are large
But she wanders the dense-leaved forests.
The bright-feathered crane rasps harshly
While the sweet-tongued cuckoo wears black.
Rivers flow with pure water,
Then the great sea turns them to salt.
Fools sit on thrones;
Wise men beg for a little naan-bread.
Mira takes the graceful Giridhara as her master.
The King hunts down the lovers of God.

Not Hiding Not Seeking

Love has stained my body
To the color of the One Who Holds Up Mountains.
When I dressed in the world's five fabrics,
I only played hide and seek—
For disguised though I was, the Lifting One caught
     me,
And seeing his beauty, I offered him all that I am.
Friends, let those whose Beloved is absent write
     letters—
Mine dwells in the heart, and neither enters nor
     leaves.
Mira has given herself to her Lord Giridhara.
Day or night, she waits only for him.

Don't Go, Don't Go

Don't go, don't go. I touch your soles. I'm sold to
you.

No one knows where to find the bhakti path, show
me where to go.

I would like my own body to turn into a heap of in-
cense and sandalwood and you set a torch to it.

When I've fallen down to gray ashes, smear me on
your shoulders and chest.

Mira says: You who lift the mountains, I have some
light, I want to mingle it with yours.

Why Mira Can't Come Back to Her Old House

The colors of the Dark One have penetrated Mira's
    body; all the other colors washed out.
Making love with the Dark One and eating little,
    those are my pearls and my carnelians.
Meditation beads and the forehead streak, those are
    my scarves and my rings.
That's enough feminine wiles for me. My teacher
    taught me this.
Approve me or disapprove me: I praise the Mountain
    Energy night and day.
I take the path that ecstatic human beings have taken
    for centuries.
I don't steal money, I don't hit anyone. What will you
    charge me with?
I have felt the swaying of the elephant's shoulders;
    and now you want me to climb on a jackass? Try
    to be serious.

The Ocean of Separation

The Necklace

O friend, I sit alone while the world sleeps.

In the palace that held love's pleasure the abandoned
one sits.

She who once threaded a necklace of pearls is now
stringing tears.

He has left me. The night passes while I count stars.

When will the Hour arrive?

This sorrow must end. Mira says: Lifter of
Mountains, return.

How This Will Go

I'm not sure, dear friend, how this will go
Between my Lord and me. My dear lover
Came to me. Then he slipped out of the courtyard,
While I, unlucky as ever, was sleeping.
I think I'll just tear my clothes in two.
I'll buy some autumn-colored robes. I'll throw my
     bracelets away
And let my hair fall around my shoulders.
I'll wash the kohl away.
What I have now is separation.
It hurts through the night and through the day.
I am sad every moment of the day.
Mirabai says: Hari, you keep stealing away. You know
Once lovers come together, they should not be kept
     apart.

The Arrow

My teacher shot an arrow, it passed all the way
    through.
Now its absence burns in my heart,
In my restless body.

My mind no longer wanders—love holds it hard.
Now I'm chained.
Who knows my pain, except him?

Helpless, unstoppable crying. Friends, tell me—what
    more can I do?

Mira says to her Lord: give me your presence or
    death.

Heading for the Ocean

Is it possible Krishna has moved to Mathuna?
His old city is empty of people.
Only the parrots are left squawking in their cages;
Even the cows are hurrying towards Mathuna.
The Jamuna riverbanks are still the same;
But one can't hear any cries from the cowherds.
I will go throw myself into the ocean,
And then I'll be reborn as Kana.
Krishna will then be reborn as Radha
And learn what it is to be abandoned.

Don't Tell Me No, Mother

Don't tell me no, Mother; I'm on my way to visit
　　holy men.

I know one with a dark face; I'm his; the rest are
　　nothing.

Where I live, everyone is sleeping; my eyes stay open
　　all night.

If the world doesn't admire the Lord, it is mad; what
　　wisdom does the world have?

What am I saying? The Lord is inside me; he's there
　　instead of sleep.

Some ponds have water only four months a year; but
　　I stay away from those ponds.

Hari's water pours down; that's good enough for my
　　thirst.

You say he is dark; I say beautiful. I am on my way to
　　see his face.

Mira's pain comes from separation; what she wants to
　　do, she'll do.

Where Did You Go?

Where did you go, Holy One, after you left my body?
Your flame jumped to the wick, and then you
  disappeared and left the lamp alone.
You put the boat into the surf, and then walked
  inland, leaving the boat in the ocean of parting.
Mira says: Tell me when you will come to meet me.

Mira Asks Only to Join with the Elephants & Parrots

O Beloved, it's promised that all who speak the Name
      will be saved.
By its power, rocks lose their hardness,
They melt like ice into water; the earth itself grows
      tender, wanting to yield.

I too feel that pull.

I've saved up no merit, know well the full weight of
      my sins.
Still, a courtesan taught her parrot to say your name
And was lifted to Vishnu's heaven.

A bathing elephant half-garbled it and you leapt to
      earth
From the back of Garuda, came running to help—
The jaws of the crocodile opened.
Releasing that elephant also from rebirth: no more
      animal wombs for him.

Ajamil named his son after you, then called the son's
    name on his deathbed.
You answered. The death-fear vanished.

Everyone knows these stories,
And you know which beings have given you their
    whole heart.
Your servant Mira asks you one question: why won't
    you save me?

Mira Is Jasmine

To love a Yogi, O Sister, is to love only sorrow.
He murmurs sweet words while he's with you,
Then forgets and departs.
For the Yogi, a sprig of jasmine
Is easily plucked, easily dropped.
Mira says to her Lord, bring back your beauty.
When I can't see you, that absence knifes open my
    heart.

The Cuckoo Calls a Beloved Who Comes

Cruel cuckoo,

Did you suddenly remember the season only to hurt
me?

I slept in my house, at last I slept—

Then your cry: "Beloved! Beloved!"

Salt to a wound. Saw-blade cutting my heart.

You perch on your branch in a high tree, singing of
love full-throated,

And Mira wakes remembering she is alone.

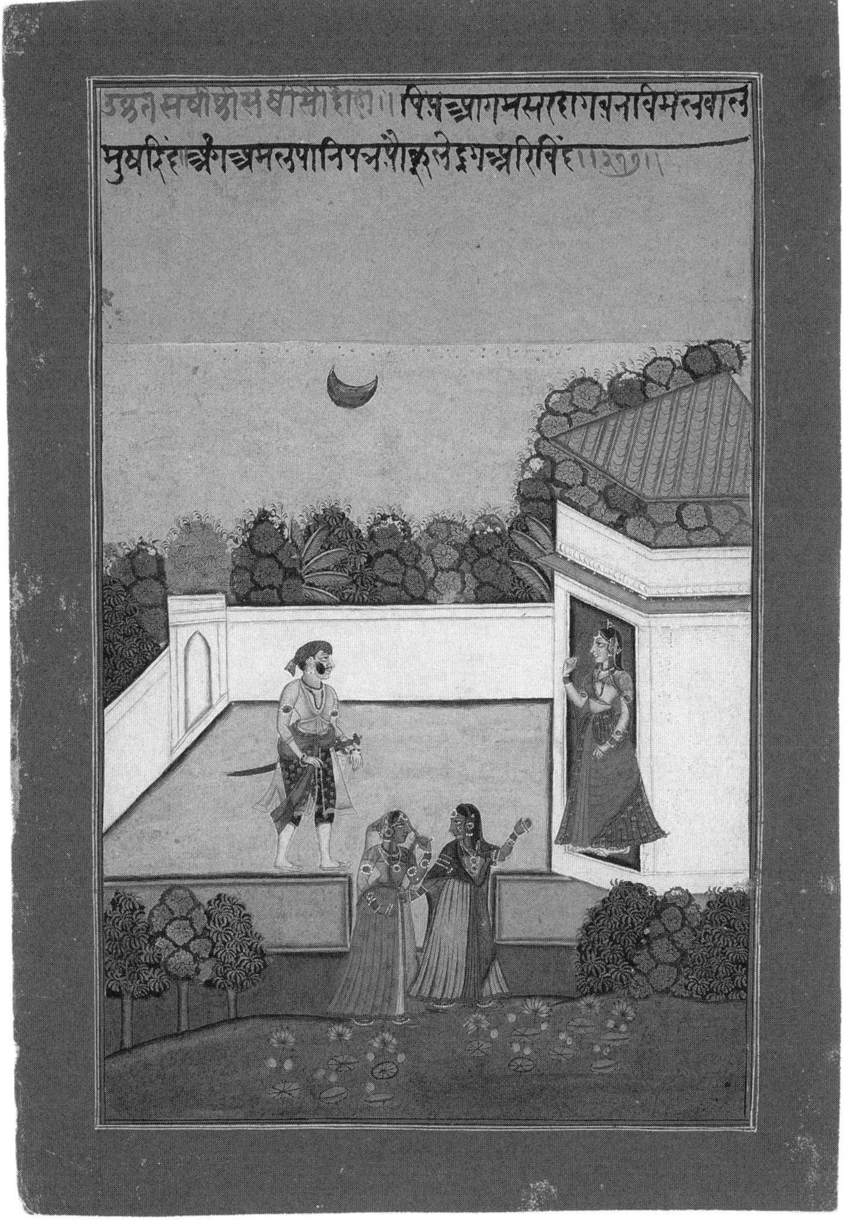

Only the Beloved Can Open
the Blossoming Spring

Without the Beloved, the festival of Holi is a bitter
   funeral.

The village grieves, the fields grieve,
The palace bed is empty.
The abandoned one wanders. Absence falls on her
   like blows.
But hunting him one place after another just fuels
   the fear.

Conquerer of Demons, come.
I've counted so many days alone my fingers grow
   callused.

Oh, I hear the castanets, the drums and flutes.
The plucked ektara sings.
Green spring has arrived. But the Beloved has not,
   and my pain grows deeper.
Why has the Dark One forgotten his lover?

Lifter of Mountains, I stand before you, I ask you to
    lift this shame.
Mira says to her Master, "Return. You are my refuge,
    body and mind.
I have slept with no other, your virgin through many
    lives."

Mira Is Mad with Love

O friends, I am mad with love, and no one sees.

My mattress is thorns, is nails:

The Beloved spreads open his bedding elsewhere.

How can I sleep? Abandonment scorches my heart.

Only those who have felt the knife can measure the
wound's deepness.

Only the jeweler knows the nature of the lost jewel.

I have lost him—

Anguish takes me from door to door, but no doctor
answers.

Mira calls her Lord: O Dark One, only you can heal
this pain.

In All My Lives

In all my lives you have been with me; whether day
or night I remember.

When you fall out of my sight, I am restless day and
night, burning.

I climb hilltops; I watch for signs of your return; my
eyes are swollen with tears.

The ocean of life—that's not genuine; the ties of
family, the obligations to the world—they're not
genuine.

It is your beauty that makes me drunk.

Mira's Lord is the Great Dark Snake. That love comes
up from the ground of the heart.

The Door

Mother, tell me why I should go on living without
    him.

When I lost him, I did go mad.

My heart resembled a door eaten out by insects.

The doctors could do nothing for me!

Some absence inside me is eating me away.

You know a fish thrown on the bank does not go on
    breathing.

It flaps its tail up and down and dies.

I go into the high trees and listen for the Dark One's
    flute.

My dear Husband and Lord, find Mira now!

The Storm Clouds

The rain clouds arrived, half mad; but I still heard
    nothing from him.
Frogs opened their mouths, peacocks shrieked,
    cuckoos and partridge sang out.
Heavy darkness came down, bolts of lightning, the
    lover felt terror in her heart.
But the wind of fragrances did come; and heavy rain
    began to fall.
The black cobra of love burns; the Storm-Bodied
    One is inside Mira's heart.

Love Has Come Home
with the Rains

Mira the Bee

O my friends,

What can you tell me of Love,

Whose pathways are filled with strangeness?

When you offer the Great One your love,

At the first step your body is crushed.

Next be ready to offer your head as his seat.

Be ready to orbit his lamp like a moth giving in to the
     light,

To live in the deer as she runs toward the hunter's
     call,

In the partridge that swallows hot coals for love of
     the moon,

In the fish that, kept from the sea, happily dies.

Like a bee trapped for life in the closing of the sweet
     flower,

Mira has offered herself to her Lord.

She says, the single Lotus will swallow you whole.

No Longer Thirsty

I was going to the river for water,
The gold pitcher balanced with care upon my head,
And Love's knife entered my heart.
Now God has bound me tightly with a fine thread,
He takes me wherever he will.
Mira's Lord is the Lifter of Mountains.
His dark beauty is all around her.

The Coffer with the Poisonous Snake

Rana sent a gold coffer of complicated ivory;
But inside a black and green asp was waiting,
"It is a necklace that belonged to a great Queen!"
I put it around my neck; it fit well.
It became a string of lovely pearls, each with a moon
    inside.
My room then was full of moonlight, as if the full
    moon
Had found its way in through the open window.

Mira the Slave

I go to the house of my one true lover, the Lifter of
    Mountains.

When I see his beauty, I only crave him more.

At dusk I go to him, at dawn I return.

Whatever his pleasure, day and night I am his.

The clothes he gives me, I wear. The food he offers,
    I eat.

Where he wants me to be, I stay. If he wants to sell
    me, I want to be sold.

Mira says, My love for Giridhara has lasted through
    many rebirths,

Without him I scarcely breathe. She offers herself to
    him in all of her lives.

Awake to the Name

To be born in a human body is rare,
Don't throw away the reward of your past good
    deeds.
Life passes in an instant—the leaf doesn't go back to
    the branch.
The ocean of rebirth sweeps up all beings hard,
Pulls them into its cold-running, fierce, implacable
    currents.
Giridhara, your name is the raft, the one safe-passage
    over.
Take me quickly.
All the awake ones travel with Mira, singing the
    name.
She says with them: Get up, stop sleeping—the days
    of a life are short.

The Long Drought Is Over

My Beloved has come home with the rains,
And the fire of longing is doused.
Now is the time for singing, the time of union.
At the first thunderclap,
Even the peacocks open their tails with pleasure and
    dance.
Giridhara is in my courtyard, and my wandering
    heart has returned.
Like lilies that blossom under the full moon's light,
I open to him in this rain: every pore of my body is
    cooled.
Mira's separation and torment are over.
He who comes to those who love has remembered
    his promise.

Near the Throne

I'm associated now with the King's court; it must
    have been some work in a previous life.
If lakes are no use to me, why should I want a pond?
The Ganga and Jamuna Rivers won't do for me; I'll
    head for the sea.
Subordinate persons are not enough; I'll talk to the
    Chief.
Wily courtiers are not for me; I'll go to the Throne.
Tin and glass break easily; so bring the iron, the heat,
    and the hammer.
Even trading in gold and silver is not for me; I bury
    my hands in diamonds.
My time of good luck is come; the ocean that stores
    jewels is nearby.
What sort of person would say no to ambrosia and
    drink stale water?
I know what holy men are like; I love them; crooked
    men I don't like.
Mira's Lord is the Dark One; I make love with him
    again and again.

Drunk for Life

Friend, listen: this love doesn't come or go.
One sip from the cup of that sweetness, the world
	starts to spin.
Now I'm a drunk for life. Unsoberable. Tell them it's
	useless to try.
King Rana sent a snake in a basket; they said, put this
	on your neck.
Princess Mira fastened that jewelry smiling, called it
	her nine-stranded pearls.
Then he concocted a poison; the household said,
	drink.
Mira gulped it like fragrant water that had bathed the
	Lord's feet.
Sing the Cowherder's praises.
If you've swallowed the Name, no other liquor can
	touch you.
Mira's Lord can lift mountains,
His love isn't some paint not worth buying, that
	comes off in the rain or the heat.

Water through the Fingers

Rana gave me poison; we all know about that.

But when gold enters the fire, it becomes purer gold.

My family's honor, my reputation—it's all water
    running through the fingers.

Add a curtain to your house; I am weak and half-mad.

An arrow from his bow hit me; now I'm certifiably
    crazy.

I've given body and soul to the saints; I hold on to
    the lotuses of their feet.

The Lord has saved Mira; he knows well that she is
    his servant.

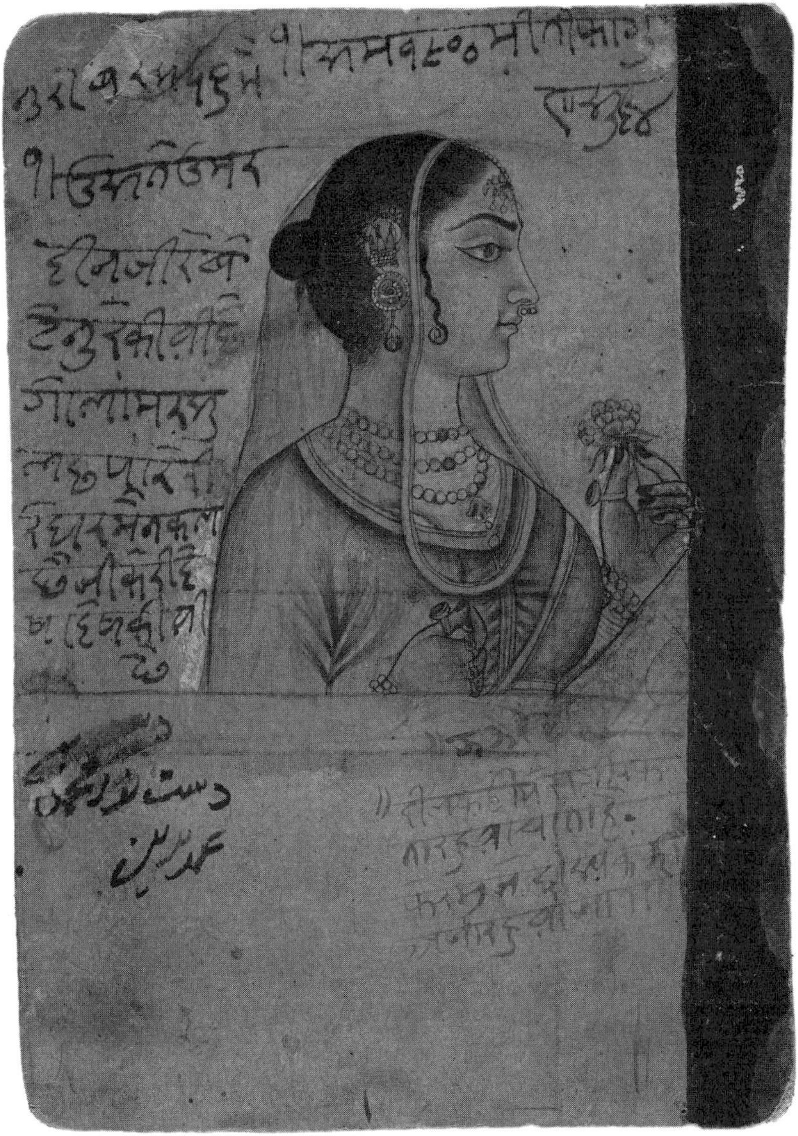

Wild Plums Are Sweetest

The wild woman of the forests
Discovered the sweet plums by tasting,
And brought them to her Lord—
She who was neither cultured nor lovely,
She who was filthy in disarrayed clothes,
She of the lowest of castes.
But the Lord, seeing her heart,
Took the ruined plums from her hand.
She saw no difference between low and high,
Wanting only the milk of his presence.
Illiterate, she never studied the teachings—
A single turn of the chariot's wheel
Brought her to knowledge.
Now she is bound to the Storm Bodied One
By gold cords of love, and wanders his woods.
Servant Mira says:
Whoever can love like this will be saved.
My Master lifts all that is fallen,
And from the beginning I have been the handmaiden
Herding cows by his side.

Mira Swims Free

What do I care for the words of the world?
The name of the Dark One has entered my heart.
Those who praise, those who blame,
Those who say I am crazy, wicked, an uncontrolled
    fire—
All ignorant fools, caught in their senses.
It is true, Mira has no sense: she is lost in the
    sweetness.
To take this path is to walk the edge of the sword;
Then the noose of birth and death is suddenly cut.
Mira lives now beyond Mira.
She swims, deep mind and deep body, in Shyam's
    ocean.

Mira the Barterer

Friend, this body is a great ocean,
Concealing reefs and sea-vaults heaped up with jewels.
Enter its secret rooms and light your own lamp.
Within the body are gardens, rare orchids, peacocks,
    the inner music.
Within the body, a lake; in its cool waters, white
    swans take their joy.
And within the body, a vast market—
Go there and trade, sell yourself for a profit you can't
    spend.
Mira says, her Lord's beauty cannot be measured.
She wants only to live near his feet.

The Clouds

When I saw the dark clouds, I wept, O Dark One,
    I wept at the dark clouds.
Black clouds soared up, and took some yellow along;
    rain did fall, some rain fell long.
There was water east of the house, west of the house;
    fields all green.
The one I love lives past those fields; rain has fallen
    on my body, on my hair, as I wait in the open
    door for him.
The Energy that holds up mountains is the energy
    Mirabai bows down to.
He lives century after century, and the test I set for
    him he has passed.

To Dance for the Dark One
Is All the Clothing Mira Needs

I am dancing only for my Master,
All I want is to please him and keep his eyes.
The gold chains I wear on my ankles are love of
    Shyam,
My dancing dress is my faithfulness to him.
I've stripped off shame and family custom
To go to the bed of the Dark One.
Body and mind, Mira wears only the color of God.

Faithfulness

My friend, he looked, and our eyes met; an arrow
    came in.

My chest opened; what could it do? His image
    moved inside.

I've been standing all morning in the door of my
    house, looking down the road.

The one I love is dark: he is an herb growing in secret
    places, an herb that heals wounds.

Mira says: The town thinks I am loose, but I am
    faithful to the Dark One.

Mira the Lotus

My Lord, the love that binds us cannot be broken.
It is hard as the diamond that shatters the hammer
    that strikes it.
As polish goes into the gold, my heart has gone into
    you.
As a lotus lives in its water, I am rooted in you.
Like the bird that gazes all night at the passing moon,
I have blinded myself in giving my eyes to your
    beauty.
She who offers herself completely asks only this:
That her Lord love Mira as fully as he is loved.

The Heat of Midnight Tears

Listen, my friend, this road is the heart opening,
Kissing his feet, resistance broken, tears all night.

If we could reach the Lord through immersion in
    water,
I would have asked to be born a fish in this life.
If we could reach him through nothing but berries and
    wild nuts
Then surely the saints would have been monkeys when
    they came from the womb!
If we could reach him by munching lettuce and dry
    leaves
Then the goats would surely get to the Holy One
    before us!

If the worship of stone statues could bring us all the way,
I would have adored a granite mountain years ago.

Mirabai says: The heat of midnight tears will bring you
    to God.

No More Drought

Today, let the rainclouds open—
Mira's Lord is at home.
Even the finest mists can fill the dry tanks,
And long searching has brought me my love.
No fear remains, no absence, no drought—
He has returned.
Mira says to her husband from previous lifetimes,
Even the cattle drink this rising water.

AFTERWORD
John Stratton Hawley

Among the poet-saints whose lives and words anchor the literature of Hindu devotion *(bhakti),* the best known and most widely loved is Mirabai. Since *bhakti* is largely a vernacular thing—the voice of experience—other poet-saints often exceed Mira's popularity in particular linguistic regions. But if you were to convene a parliament of those regions and call for a vote on who qualifies as Greatest Saint Ever, it's likely that Mirabai would win the election. Her story is told from one end of India to the other, and more or less unceasingly in her native Rajasthan. At least ten movies have been made about her life, and her persona shapes the behavior of heroines who appear in many other films, religious and nonreligious alike.[1] She's the subject of countless academic conferences; she was also the first *bhakti* saint to make it into the "classics illustrated" *Amar Chitra Katha* comic-book series, which is devoured by Hindu children everywhere.[2] An international conference held at UCLA in 2002 hailed her as "Hindu Saint for a Global World," and in this volume Robert Bly and Jane Hirshfield make it clear that they too feel her magnetism.

But who is Mirabai? Of all the *bhakti* poets of North India, none is more familiar on the basis of her life story, yet none is more mysterious when it comes to ferreting out what she actually said, sang, and did. Many of her sixteenth-century peers have left a substantial research trail, thanks to manuscripts where their songs are collected, but Mira is almost invisible. How many Mira poems— compositions bearing her oral signature—can be said with complete confidence to have circulated in her own century? One.[3]

As we will see, it is plain that her life story was well known by the end of the sixteenth century, yet her poetry was never included in the early anthologies. Was it because she was a woman? Because she was a member of no sect, and no sect claimed her? Or was it that very little poetry bearing her name was in fact composed that early on, despite her reputation as an ecstatic singer? We simply don't know. Yet one thing is sure: all these questions haven't stopped the tradition of Mirabai poetry from growing and flowering in more recent centuries. The beautiful renditions crafted for this volume are the latest crest on a long, long wave of poetry associated with her name.

The Mirabai Story

If the poetry has shaky historical moorings, the story that circulated about her life in the sixteenth and seventeenth centuries stands on much firmer ground. Indeed, the story undoubtedly had a lot to do with producing the poetry as the centuries passed. Much more than for any other North Indian poet-saint, the poems attributed to Mirabai focus on her life. It is important, then, to examine how Mirabai's story was told in the earliest versions that have come down to us.

Principally, there are two of these, one from the Punjab and the other from Rajasthan. The first is found in the *Prem Abodh* ("On Love"), a hagiographical collection for which we have a manuscript dating to 1783; it in turn tells us it is a copy of a manuscript dated 1693. The *Prem Abodh*'s section on Mirabai is suffused with an aura of devotional fervor that swirls around some of the most celebrated features of her life story. We hear how she achieved union with Krishna, "opening the door" to him in night-long vigils; how she became, in a way, his priest—and was hated by her family for taking on this public role; how her public presence made her a target for sexual assault by one of her religious colleagues, a man whose prayers and holy robes served as cover for a body seething with desire; and finally, how she emerged victorious from a head-to-head confrontation with the forces of social propriety enshrined in her own family. In this last section—the climax, from the *Prem Abodh*'s point of view—we find Mira arrayed against the *rana,* the Rajasthani king whose life was supposed to set the confines for hers.

This sounds very familiar to anyone who has heard of Mirabai, but in fact the story diverges dramatically from the account that later became standard. In the *Prem Abodh* the evil *rana* is understood not as Mira's husband or any in-law, but as her own father, a man driven to distraction by his daughter's amorous excesses. The *Prem Abodh* contains no mention of Mira's ever passing into another family by marriage, and in the absence of the motif of marital struggle the dimensions of Mira's confrontation with the *rana* actually expand. It's not just about resisting sex and the mandates of patriarchy; it's about taking a stand against the things of this world altogether. Her pellucid inner spirituality is contrasted with *samsara*—the cravings and deceptions of the external world.[4]

To emerge victorious in this confrontation, Mira did not have to rely entirely on her own resources. In the *Prem Abodh,* as elsewhere, the hero who sustains her unshakable inner certainty is the man she loves. This is Giridhar, the young Krishna who scooped up Mount Govardhan and supported it on the palm of one hand—indeed, on one finger of one hand, as some versions tell it. His purpose in doing so was to shelter the cowherds and milkmaids of his pastoral Braj homeland against the stormy assaults of Indra, captain of the ancient Vedic pantheon. Indra's ire had been kindled when Krishna—God disguised as a simple cowherd boy—suggested that the people of Braj abandon their self-alienating Vedic religion and turn their attentions instead toward the nourishing core of their actual life and livelihood: Mount Govardhan, the center and heart of the Braj countryside. Later in the story it emerges that Mount Govardhan is a physical expression of Krishna himself, who is the immovable, earth-centering presence that gives the world its prosperity and stability.[5]

So the Govardhan story celebrates the power of inner, personal religion—what today we might call spirituality—as against the random tyrannies and caprices of externalized, "organized" religion. When Mira devotes herself to Giridhar, the hero who lifts *(dhar)* the mountain *(giri),* and arrays him against her husband and in-laws, she extends the story of the struggle between intimate religion and its lifeless exterior counterpart a step further. In her, as a romantic heroine, the celebration of interior religion becomes a story that adulates personal and specifically feminine feeling.

The *Prem Abodh*'s top-heavy spirituality sometimes gets in the way of a straightforward recounting of her story: it's assumed that hearers and readers already know it. But we can get a sense of how Mira's story might have been more simply told in this early period by turning to another document and its commentary. The core text is a hagiographical anthology called the *Bhaktamal* ("A Garland of Saints"), which was composed in a monastery near Amber (modern-day Jaipur) in Rajasthan not long after 1600 C.E. The *Bhaktamal* is a string of short lyrics, probably intended to be performed in gatherings praising the lives of these saints. Its commentary, which fills out the details, is called the *Bhaktirasabodhini* ("Awakening the Mood of Love"). It was composed in 1712 by a certain Priyadas in the town of Vrindaban (a.k.a. Brindavan, Vrindavan), located some seventy-five miles south of Delhi, not far from Mount Govardhan. Going further than the *Prem Abodh* and diverging from it in certain important respects, Priyadas provides us with our first full narrative of Mira's life; Nabhadas, writing a century earlier than either, gives us the kernel.[6]

Like most subsequent biographers, Nabhadas presents Mira as a woman so absorbed in the love of Krishna that she vividly replicated the devotion of the cowherding women and girls *(gopis)* who peopled Krishna's sempiternal landscape in Braj. The *gopis* had husbands. But even if they had dedicated themselves to the lifelong service of their mates—their "husband-gods" *(patidev),* as the Hindu expression tellingly puts it—they instantly abandoned the demands of conventional morality at the sound of Krishna's flute. They dropped their brooms, churning sticks, and cooking implements, and even slipped away from the conjugal bed itself, to rush out into the forest to dance the dance of love, Krishna's circular *(ras)* dance. Mira's urge was the same: to seek out the company of quite a different "family" from that to which *dharma* had assigned her—a family composed of those who sang the praises of her Lord. This put her constantly at loggerheads with that family's earthly rival.

In its telegraphic way, Nabhadas's *Bhaktamal* sets forth the major themes that Mira's life displays:

> Modesty in public, the chains of family life—
>> Mira shed both for the Lifter of Mountains.
> Like a latter-day *gopi,* she showed what love can mean
>> in our devastated, age-ending age.
> No inhibitions. Totally fearless.
>> Her tongue sang the fame of her tasteful Lord.
> Villains thought it vile. They set out to kill her,
>> but not a single hair on her head was harmed:
> The poison she was brought turned elixir in her throat.

She cringed before none. She beat love's drum.
Modesty in public, the chains of family life —
Mira shed both for the Lifter of Mountains.[7]

The first two lines set up an opposition between conventional modesty (as defined by family bonds) and singing of Krishna, and the next two confirm that Mira's life displays the tension that the *gopis* experienced, but on an earthly plane, or rather, as the Hindu concept has it, in the degenerate world-age *(kali yug)* of which we are a part. Mention is made of the fearless, shameless quality of Mira's personality, which is presented as if it emerged in her singing. The poem then cites the great example of Mira's fearlessness: the episode in which she gladly drank the poison that her father or husband or in-laws served up to her. As if in consequence of her fearlessness, the poison turned to ambrosia in her throat. The poem concludes in the same vein, making a second reference to her outspoken *bhakti* musicianship (she is said to have beaten the great annunciatory *nisan* drum) and drawing attention again to its effect: it snapped the chains of ordinary morality.

The rest of the account—the part added by Priyadas—fleshes out the details, and in ways that sometimes contrast with the *Prem Abodh*. We are told that as a child in her father's house in the princely state of Merta, in Rajasthan, Mira fell deeply in love with Giridhar. When she was betrothed to an unspecified *rana* from another state and followed him around the marriage fire, the mantras she said in her heart were all directed to her other husband, the Mountain-Lifter. Instead of a dowry to take with her to her new home, she asked only for Him, the image of Krishna to which she had become so attached. And when she arrived at her in-laws' house, she refused to bow her head to her mother-in-law, as Hindu custom prescribes, or to the goddess who was the chosen deity of the household into which she had married. Her mother-in-law was humiliated; the *rana* was put to shame; and her behavior cast discredit on the honor of her own father's lineage as well. All family bonds were threatened by Mira's sense of having already offered herself to Krishna.

But that did not mean Mira was left with no family at all. Though her earthly family would rather poison than nourish her, Mira retained another family in "the company of the saints" *(sadhu sang)* who were, as Priyadas says, "attached to the will of Shyam," that is, Krishna. Her sister-in-law tried to dissuade her from associating with such *sadhus,* but to no avail, and the *rana,* on hearing the news, dispatched a cup of poison. He sent this poison in the guise of a liquid offering *(caranamrt,* "feet-nectar") to the feet of Krishna, Mira's deity, knowing she was bound to consume whatever was left over from the table of her divine Lord. But ironically, as she drank it, the poison became exactly the "immortal liquid from his feet" that the term *caranamrt* implies. It made her glow with greater health and happiness than before. Even her singing improved.

In the section that follows, the *Bhaktirasabodhini* takes a closer look at the nature of Mira's chosen family—the company of *sadhus.* First, the *sadhus* who customarily gather around her stop coming, which saddens her but shows that not even those who pass their lives singing of God always possess the fearlessness such a life requires. Mira is left with only Krishna for her family of faith. But the departure of the *sadhus* is providential, since at that time the *rana* extends his murderous jealousy from Mira to any with whom she might speak. It has been rumored that she has liaisons with other men. Indeed someone overhears her cooing to a lover behind her door. The *rana* is summoned, appears hastily with sword in hand, demands to be admitted to her chamber, and asks her to show him the man with whom she has been conversing so lovingly. Her response is to tell him that the one he seeks is standing directly in front of him—her image of Krishna—and that he is not one to shy away from an encounter. The *rana,* flustered and angry, freezes "like a picture on the wall" and retreats.

Thus it is he, her "true" husband, who fearfully flees, not the one who appears to worldly eyes her paramour, her illegitimate consort. And the way in which the *rana* goes deepens the sense of irony that Priyadas delights in conveying. He, though flesh and blood, turns stonelike, a mere image of reality, when faced with the image who is so much more than an image—"real life" itself.

The next episode provides yet another instance of Mira's fearlessness, and again the battle is fought over the issue of marital fidelity and sexual propriety. This time Mira is truly faced with a vile and dissolute would-be lover, a man who comes to her in the guise of a *sadhu* and urges her to submit to his advances on the strength of the claim that Giridhar himself has commanded it. We meet him in the *Prem Abodh* as well. We learn nothing about sagacity or credulity from Mira's response to this gentleman; for Priyadas the lesson has to do, once again, with an absence of fear. Mirabai simply replies that she accepts Giridhar's orders in all humility, and with that she offers the man food and has a bed made.

But she goes him one better. She lays out the bower in the presence of her musical congregation, urging on the lecher the same fearlessness that is by now her trademark: in that open, communal context she urges him to have good fun as well—another Krishna-like virtue. The result is that it is he, not she, who fears and feels shame. He blanches, loses any desire for corporeal contact, and begs her to help him attain the godly devotion that she displays.

Thus Mira's place in the "community of saints" is tested from without (by the *rana*) and within (by the false *sadhu*), and in both cases it is her absence of shame in the presence of Krishna that makes her defenselessness a true defense. By breathing the expansive magnanimity of her Lord, she shames the shameless.

By the same token she charms the great. The Mughal emperor Akbar, a frequent figure in hagiographies of the time, is drawn from afar to hear her sing. Accompanied by his chief musician, Tansen, he comes into Mira's presence disguised as a commoner, which teaches that neither rank nor religious affiliation (Akbar is a Muslim) is relevant to religious community. Before long Tansen is moved to song.

Yet not everyone is so impervious to issues of status and boundary as Akbar, even within the *bhakti* community itself. In the next episode Mira travels to Vrindaban, the town established in the sixteenth century to memorialize Krishna's *ras* dance and the hub of Krishna worship in Braj. There she is refused an audience with one of the town's leading figures, the theologian Jiv Gosvami. Jiv shrinks from a meeting with Mira because he has vowed never to have concourse with a woman, but Mira quickly sets him straight. She reminds him that in Vrindaban there is really only one male, Krishna. All the rest are *gopis* before him. The lesson, once again, is that religious community is an open reality, devoid of the marks of hierarchy. Fear and modesty have no place there.

Mira's last journey takes her to Dvaraka, the temple town on the shore of the Arabian Sea that serves as the most impressive focus for Krishna worship in western India. She hopes that under its influence her service to Giridhar may be deepened one final measure. When she has been gone for some time, the *rana* finally misses her and recognizes that she is the very personification of *bhakti*, of love. Perhaps the lesson is that even the world of profane morality cannot survive forever without the higher dimension that Mira represents. The *rana* sends a delegation of Brahmins to persuade her to return, but she refuses. Driven to extremes, they try to win her back with a hunger strike, which does indeed earn her sympathy, but Krishna himself prevents her departure. One day, as she worships in the temple, he draws her into his own image, and she is never seen again. The story ends, thus, on an ambiguous note. Mira may be willing to explore the possible coexistence of earthly propriety and heavenly devotion—exterior and interior religion—but Krishna, the great hero of music and antistructure, cannot bear to see her try.

This is the true denouement of Mira's adventurous life as told by Priyadas, but he saves one crucial aspect for another story—his account of the life of the poet-saint, Ravidas. Ravidas was a shoemaker who lived in Banaras, someone who worked with leather, and his daily, physical contact with the skin of dead animals relegated him to a place near the bottom of India's caste hierarchy. But Ravidas was also a famous singer, and the story goes that he was paid a visit by a queen of the Jhali lineage from Rajasthan—a shadow, perhaps, of Mirabai. This queen was in search of a guru, and much to the consternation of the Brahmins in her entourage, she found him in the "untouchable" cobbler of Banaras. Priyadas does not use Mira's name in this context—he cannot, since he locates the queen in a separate lineage—but many other writers, the earliest being the author of the *Prem Abodh,* have prized this connection and made it clear.

The idea that royalty would seek spiritual counsel from the lowest reaches of society has remained very much alive in the Mirabai tradition. When the sociologist Parita Mukta sought out the Mira celebrated among itinerant singers and lower-caste people in western Rajasthan and neighboring Gujarat, she found this Mirabai at the core of things. For them, it was not just a rejection of patriarchal conventions when Mira snubbed the *rana,* but a rejection of social injustice broadly—of caste.[8]

Not surprisingly, this element is apt to be absent in a third venerable source to which Mira's devotees often appeal in their efforts to discover who she was: historical records associated with the royal families of Rajasthan. Here the going gets a little rough, though you would never know it from all that has been claimed and published. The problem is that royal genealogies focus exclusively on males, so there is no reason for Mirabai to appear in these genealogical accounts, and this problem is intensified by the fact that everything in her story requires her to be childless—that is, sonless. So by that route too, she misses any possibility of being entered into the royal record.

Everyone takes it for granted that the family into which Mira married was that of the kings of Mewar, where the title *rana* is best known. Priyadas heads us in this direction with his tale of the Jhali queen from Chittor, capital of Mewar, but does not actually close the loop and say that this Jhali queen is Mirabai. Thus an element of mystery remains, and it is not removed by the old Mewari histories. They contain no mention of Mirabai. It's the same with the archaeological and inscriptional record: various traces of a Mira-Mewar connection have been claimed, but none holds up to rigorous scrutiny.

The one time Mira emerges in an early official document is in Munhata Nainsi's royal history of Jodhpur, not far from her natal Merta, which was written in the middle of the seventeenth century. There, indeed, we hear that Mirabai was married into the royal family of Mewar. The husband claimed for her is a certain Bhojraj, one of the sons of the well-known monarch Rana Sanga, and since the late nineteenth century, at least, this marriage has been accepted as historical fact.[9] But there is a difficulty. All Nainsi really says is that people *say* Mirabai was married to Bhojraj; he departs from his normal discourse to insert this verb.[10]

Of course, even if he's only reporting hearsay, not the product of any royal record, that in itself is important. Rumor it may be, but it's a seventeenth-century rumor. Yet the historical thread is thin. Mirabai does not otherwise figure in any dynastic account written within a century or so of her own approximate lifetime, and the remainder of her story is simply missing. It has no place in this sort of record; she does not make her debut in actual chronicles of Mewar until the nineteenth century.[11]

Playing Mira's Song

As for the poems associated with Mirabai, they are even harder to find in old manuscripts. Odd ones appear here and there, but only rarely, with the result that scholars today have counted at most some twenty-five poems attributed to Mira in manuscripts dating up to the end of the seventeenth century. The great bulk of these compositions—sixteen poems—are said to exist in three mid-seventeenth-century manuscripts housed at the Gujarat Vidya Sabha in Ahmedabad, but all three manuscripts are either lost or misplaced. In the present state of scholarship we have access to only six poems that we know were sung in Mira's name before the end of the seventeenth century. Of these, intriguingly, only one has made its way into today's most frequently consulted collections. And since Robert Bly and Jane Hirshfield draw on precisely those collections, none of the certifiably early poems—the ones we might most reasonably associate with a historical Mirabai—figure in this book. The Mira we meet here is much more modern than most of her devotees have any reason to know—she is a nineteenth-century Mira at best—and the same can be said for oral and written editions that circulate in India itself.

On the face of it, perhaps we should regret the profound disconnect between the historical Mirabai, whoever she was, and the poetry recited in her name. But let's look at it a different way. This radical disjuncture makes it clear that the poetry has a life of its own, constantly developing and changing, a cloud that floats freely above the surface of the earth. Air is an element too, after all—not just "historical" earth with its strata and plates and molten underpinnings—and this air of collective memory breeds its own forms.

Shall we call it love? The huge, ongoing Mirabai corpus—I use the term advisedly—breathes that substance, and may even have taken its first life-breath there: not in history (when was love ever constrained by the facts?) but against history, in the struggle of an ideal love against the limitations of the earthly vessels constructed to receive, obscure, and dilute it. Mirabai means romance in the pure sense, romance understood as divine. For twenty-first-century Americans the media—first and foremost film—may provide the easiest way to understand the medium in which Mirabai has always thrived. She is elemental in a mediated way, but that doesn't make her less real. To the contrary, it makes her *more* real.

Mirabai's power through the centuries contrasts completely with that of her fellow Indian ecstatic poet, Kabir. However many "Kabirs" have composed verse in his name—in his key—it's almost impossible to think of the earthy grittiness that is his signature without conceiving of it as rooted initially in the wit and trenchancy of a particular historical individual. Not Mira. For all the force of the story that pits her against the king to beat all kings, the *rana* of Mewar, this is an archetypal confrontation, not a historical one. As we've seen, the deepest historical roots of the Mirabai story don't sink themselves convincingly into Mewari earth. Of course, latter-day historians have tried to shore up these foundations, but the historical ties are not what makes the story live. It's the story's archetypal power—the Ur-Woman arrayed against all those powerful men and the structures they create to keep her in her place. Her organic link to spirit keeps her safe from the many structure-focused men. This spirit is the Mountain-Lifter, and despite the busy efforts of those same latter-day historians, he too floats above the shrapnel of history.

We need to know the genealogy of stories and poems gathered in Mira's name, and a main purpose of this essay is to try to spell them out. Yet the ultimate purpose of learning these truths is not to fasten them onto her work, but to see how they set us, her readers, free. The search for the historical Mirabai shows us that in the end, she lives in a different realm.

On the whole, the same can be said for her poetry. If you read it in the "original"—in Hindi, on the page—the force of individual words and phrases tends to be far less compelling than what one meets in verse attributed to many other poets of her generation and ilk. Certainly these words are less interesting and tart than those we associate with Kabir, and far less artful than the words of someone like Surdas or Bihari. But liberate them from the page and into speech, and then out of speech and into song, and perhaps out of song into cinema, and you find yourself in the world where Mirabai truly thrives. She's a sung reality; and if seen, she's seen with that inner eye that puts her eternally onstage—wrapped in a gossamer white sari, plucking away at the single string of the world's simplest instrument, and lost in a haze of Krishna. No wonder she's so eternally available to shore up the suffering heroines of this or that just-released Hindi film: they have only to assume her pose. If Krishna and *gopis* are her aura, then she, by the same token, becomes theirs. Mirabai is eternally available for projection.

Against this background it makes sense that Robert Bly and Jane Hirshfield should give us a Mirabai deeply colored by their own vision of who she was, and by their estimation of how poems in the Mirabai "cloud" can best precipitate for readers of contemporary English, especially American ones. These are "versions," they tell us, rather than translations. If it's been necessary to supply a phrase to enable a poem to speak to English readers, they have added it in good conscience. In the well-known poem where Mira dreams her marriage to Krishna, for instance, we hear that "all the doorways were made royal" and that "all my relatives were there." I can see how royal doorways might emerge as a general interpretation of the word *toran,* though the poet is actually referring to a specific ornament placed atop a single ritual arch in front of the bride's house so that the groom, arriving on horseback, can touch it with his conquering sword. But the phrase about the relatives is absent in the original; it's been added to fill out the scene for Western readers.[12]

Does this ahistorical approach to Mirabai somehow lack legitimacy? Not at all. Since the whole poetic corpus attributed to Mirabai is quite divorced from any rooting in her own time, there is good reason to approach the poems with the expectation that they have fed and will feed actively on the creativity of others—people just like Robert Bly and Jane Hirshfield. Rich Freeman has recently urged the point that "in Kerala text-artifacts were often merely scripts for improvisation."[13] The same is often true for many North Indian *bhakti* poets, and truer for Mirabai than most.

In the Bly-Hirshfield versions, plenty of room has been left for improvisation. One sees it in the captivating titles they provide, since the original poems have none: for instance, the notion of Mira being "drunk for life," as the title of one poem proclaims, or of "the gooseberry patch," as in the title and text of another. This is a little like Rogier van der Weyden painting a Flemish background for an icon of Mary and Jesus, thereby helping viewers imagine the biblical scene as real, belonging to their own world. But what about instances where it isn't just scenery? What about the idea that the central persona of Krishna to whom Mira appeals is "Mountain Energy" or the "Energy that holds up mountains"? There's no "energy" in any original (or better, perhaps, copy-text) of which I am aware, but Robert Bly must have felt that the whole motif of a divine adolescent lifting a mountain ought to suggest the displacement of matter into its dynamic counterpart: $E = mc^2$. A fundamental transformation like this is invisible to most readers and perhaps, therefore, misleading. But it is not without a deep, intriguing logic.

Let's go a further step. Consider the figure Bly and Hirshfield call the "Great Dark Snake," who sometimes gets joined to this mountain-lifting presence as "the

Great Snake Giridhar"? This happens, for instance, in the poem called "A Dream of Marriage," about which we were just speaking. I have to confess I can't follow this usage back to its interpolative source—it's certainly not in the original. Could it possibly be an interpretation of the word *nāgar,* which does indeed appear along with the word *giridhar* in the epithet Mira most frequently assigns to Krishna? If so, I'd have to say that by my lights, at least, to render it as "Great Snake" is a mistake. A *nāg* is a snake, yes, a cobra, but the word *nāgar,* meaning "clever" or "urbane," is derived by another route altogether—from *nagar* (without the long mark), meaning "city." It connotes grace and refinement, and I'm not sure how that could bleed over into a sense of the serpentine.

Yet on the whole these versions' special twists do supply seasoning in just the way that spices ought to do. They bring out the flavor of the original—that is, the original as understood within the cumulative tradition of performance that has made it what it is. Let me mention two examples that appear in these poets' rendering of one of the most famous poems in the Mirabai repertoire, *jogi mat ja mat ja,* translated here as "Don't Go, Don't

Go."[14]As is easy to see, the first word in the poem—*jogi,* a yogi—has simply been omitted. In its Hindi form the whole poem is addressed to Krishna in his yogi persona, but we only catch on to this fact when we read into the body of the poem, where Bly alludes to people who smear themselves with "gray ashes." Bly drops this notion of a yogi from the opening line, preferring an unmediated discourse. With no delimitation whatever, the speaker pleads with her lover, "Don't go, don't go." It's the same at the end, where she says, ever so directly, "I have some light, I want to mingle it with yours." Here we have an addition rather than an omission. There's no "I want" in the original; it merely says, "Merge my light with yours." But to Bly this verb of desiring must have seemed the best way to get across the directness and urgency of the original utterance, even at the cost of shifting the agency from the person addressed to the person doing the addressing—from Krishna to Mirabai.

This sense of urgency and directness is a signal feature of the "versions" that Bly and Hirshfield give us. As a group, they are less about Krishna than Mirabai, who emerges as a regular paradigm of subjectivity, a subject's subject. These are poems of experience, of personhood. Any sense of Krishna as an image is gone. To enter Mira's realm, he must be absolute reality—Energy, a subject's reality, rather than an independent mass. This is some distance from the sort of Krishna who could be associated with the Giridhar statue Mira is said to have brought with her to her wedding ceremony, the one Priyadas says displaced her husband. Translating for a world that doesn't command that sort of ease with images, Bly and Hirshfield have paved a new road. It involves some innovation, no doubt, and readers who wonder what it took to create such bypasses will have to compare these versions with other, more literal translations. But the result, I would argue, is faithful to the way that Mira has very often been understood in India itself: totally in love, utterly devoted, single-minded in her speech, simple in tone, straighter than straight.

"Don't go, don't go." For most contemporary English readers, especially those living outside India, this detour from the original turns out to be a straightening of the road. It says, in another way, "Go!" The Bly-Hirshfield versions do very little in the way of surrounding Mirabai with *sadhus,* sisters, and other believers, the way Priyadas did. They are not very interested in community. Instead they strive for an unfiltered, personal vision, and in doing so, perhaps they take us a step back behind Priyadas—to his mentor, Nabhadas. Nabha's Mira was nothing if she was not fearless, and these translations are very much in that spirit. They are fearless, too.

NOTES

1. Philip Lutgendorf, "The 'Mira Trope' in Mainstream Hindi Cinema: Three Examples from Notable Films," paper delivered to the international conference on Mirabai held at the University of California at Los Angeles, 4 October 2002, and forthcoming in Nancy M. Martin, ed., *Mirabai: Hindu Saint for a Global World.*

2. See chapter 6, "The Saints Subdued in *Amar Chitra Katha,*" in my *Three Bhakti Voices: Mirabai, Surdas, and Kabir in Their Time and Ours* (Delhi: Oxford University Press, 2005).

3. Found in the *Kartārpur Bīr* of 1604, a forerunner of the *Gurū Granth Sāhib,* the Sikh scriptural anthology; translated and analyzed in Hawley, *Three Bhakti Voices,* chapter 4, "Mirabai in Manuscript." Also Winand M. Callewaert, "The 'Earliest' Song of Mira (1503–1546)," *Journal of the Oriental Institute* (University of Baroda) 39 (1990), p. 376, note 17; C. L. Prabhāt, *Mīrāṅbāī (Śodh Prabandh)* (Bombay: Hindī Granth Ratnākar, 1965), p. 245, and *Mīrā: Jīvan aur Kāvya* (Jodhpur: Rājasthānī Granthāgār, 1999), pp. 462–469; Nancy M. Martin, *Mirabai* (New York: Oxford University Press, forthcoming). An entire manuscript of Mirabai poetry has been claimed as bearing a sixteenth-century date, but that claim is almost surely false. See Paul B. Arney, "The Dakor and Kashi Manuscripts: Are They Genuine?" (unpublished paper, Columbia University, 1989), and other writings reviewed in Hawley, *Three Bhakti Voices,* chapter 4.

4. Devindar Siṃh Usāhaṇ, *Prem Abodh* (Patiala: Panjabi University Publication Bureau, 1989), pp. 109, 115, *chaupaīs* 3, 4, cf. 22.

5. See my "A Feast for Mount Govardhan," in Diana L. Eck and Françoise Mallison, eds., *Devotion Divine: Bhakti Traditions from the Regions of India* [*Festschrift* for Charlotte Vaudeville] (Groningen: Egbert Forsten and Paris: École Française d'Extrême Orient, 1991), pp. 155–179.

6. Nābhādās et al., *Śrī Bhaktamāl,* with the *Bhaktirasabodhinī* commentary of Priyādās, ed. Bhagavān Prasād Rūpakalā (Lucknow: Tejkumār Press, 1969 [originally 1910]).

7. Nābhādās, *Bhaktamāl,* pp. 712–713.

8. Parita Mukta, *Upholding the Common Life: The Community of Mirabai* (Delhi: Oxford University Press, 1994), pp. 90–112. This presents a direct contrast to the *Prem Abodh,* which specifies on two occasions that Mira does not reject caste but instead lauds the four *varṇas* (Usāhaṇ, *Prem Abodh,* pp. 114, 117, *chaupaīs* 20, 28).

9. See Nancy Martin, "Mirabai in the Academy and the Politics of Identity," in Mandakranta Bose, ed., *Faces of the Feminine from Ancient, Medieval, and Modern India* (New York: Oxford University Press, 2000), pp. 169–171.

10. "Bhojrāj Sāṅgāvat: they say that Mīrābāī Rāthor was married to him" *(bhojarāja sāṅgāvata / iṇanuṅ kahe chai mīrāṅbāī rāṭhoḍa paraṇāī hutī).* In Muṅhatā Naiṇsī, *Muṅhatā Naiṇsī rī Khyāt,* vol. 1, ed. Badarīprasād Sākariyā (Jodhpur: Rājasthānī Prācyavidyā Pratiṣṭhān, 1960), p. 21.

11. A careful analysis of the overall process by means of which a picture of Mirabai gradually developed on the basis of dynastic sources has been made by Frances Taft, "The Elusive Histori-

cal Mirabai: A Note," in Lawrence A. Babb, Varsha Joshi, and Michael Meister, eds., *Multiple Histories, Culture, and Society in the Study of Rajasthan* (Jaipur: Rawat Publications, 2002), pp. 313–335. For a very different—and to me persuasive—perspective, against which Taft is arguing, see Nancy Martin, "Mirabai in the Academy," pp. 162–182. Worth comparing in matters of substance, but different in style and presuppositions from either of these, is Kalyāṇsiṃh Śekhāvat's *Mīrāṅ kī Prāmāṇik Jīvanī* (Jodhpur: Rājasthānī Granthāgār, 2002). I review several salient details in *Three Bhakti Voices,* chapter 4.

12. Paraśurām Caturvedī, ed., *Mīrāṅbāī kī Padāvalī* (Allahabad: Hindī Sāhitya Sammelan, 1973 [originally 1932], poem no. 27.

13. This summary evaluation emerges in Sheldon Pollock's introduction to his edited volume, *Literary Cultures in History: Reconstructions from South Asia* (Berkeley: University of California Press, 2004), p. 22.

14. E.g., Caturvedī, *Mīrāṅbāī kī Padāvalī,* poem no. 46.

TRANSLATOR CREDITS

All I Was Doing Was Breathing—RB

The Dagger—RB

Mira Has Finished with Waiting—JH

It's True I Went to the Market—RB

Mira the Milkmaid—JH

The Fish and the Crocodile—RB

Polish into Gold—JH

A Dream of Marriage—RB

Ankle Bells—RB

The Flute—JH

The Rope of Jasmine Blossoms—RB

His Hair—RB

The Gooseberry Patch—RB

To My Brother-in-Law Rana—RB

Fate Is Strange—JH

Not Hiding Not Seeking—JH

Don't Go, Don't Go—RB

Why Mira Can't Come Back to Her Old House—
RB

The Necklace—JH

How This Will Go—RB

The Arrow—JH

Heading for the Ocean—RB

Don't Tell Me No, Mother – RB

Where Did You Go?—RB

Mira Asks Only to Join with the Elephants &
    Parrots—JH

Mira Is Jasmine—JH

The Cuckoo Calls a Beloved Who Comes—JH

Only the Beloved Can Open the Blossoming
    Spring—JH

Mira Is Mad with Love—JH

In All My Lives—RB

The Door—RB

The Storm Clouds—RB

Mira the Bee – JH

No Longer Thirsty—JH

The Coffer with the Poisonous Snake—RB

Mira the Slave—JH

Awake to the Name—JH

The Long Drought Is Over—JH

Near the Throne—RB

Drunk for Life—JH

Water through the Fingers—RB

Wild Plums Are Sweetest—JH

Mira Swims Free—JH

Mira the Barterer—JH

The Clouds—RB

To Dance for the Dark One Is All the Clothing
    Mira Needs—JH

Faithfulness—RB

Mira the Lotus—JH

The Heat of Midnight Tears—RB

No More Drought—JH & RB